THE CHINES

THE CHINESE DRAGON

90-YEAR ANNIVERSARY EDITION

BY L. NEWTON HAYES

THE FIRST ENGLISH BOOK EVER PUBLISHED ON THIS MAGNIFICENT CREATURE

THE CHINESE DRAGON

90-YEAR ANNIVERSARY EDITION

By L. Newton Hayes

The first English book ever published on this magnificent creature.

With an Introduction by

Fong F. SEC, LL.D.

Fourth Edition Revisions by

K. Rubacek

First Printed in 1922

Reprinted in 1922, 1923, 2012

Copyright © Kay Rubacek, 2012. All rights reserved. No part of this book may be reproduced in any form, except brief excerpts for the purpose of review without written permission of the publisher.

Cover image: Emperor Kangxi, surrounded by dragons upon his robe and the imperial throne.

www.TheChineseDragonBook.com

ISBN: 978-1-105-47865-9

THE 90-YEAR ANNIVERSARY EDITION OF THIS BOOK IS DEDICATED TO ALL WHO HAVE NOT FORGOTTEN THEIR CULTURAL HERITAGE AND BELIEFS.

For further information, news and sightings on
The Chinese Dragon, please visit:

www.TheChineseDragonBook.com

龍騰九洲五千載
庇佑中華不遭邪
誰料西來紅卷風
吹却國人敬神念
二零一二年三月三日承行

Five thousand years in guarding

For China dragons were prevailing

Suddenly entered the red cyclone from the West

People's respect of the divine has dwindled

CUIYING ZHANG

CHINESE ARTIST, 2012

BRONZE DRAGON, KANGXI PERIOD

Four hundred years ago Pero Veribest, Jesuit priest at the court of Kangxi (formerly romanized as Kang Hsi), cast a number of bronze astronomical instruments for his imperial patron. The apparatus, of which this is a part, stands in the open, but the workmanship is so perfect and the care it has received has been so faithful that one would hardly imagine that this dragon was cast more than four centuries ago.

CONTENTS

ILLUSTRATIONS 11

EDITOR'S NOTE 14

INTRODUCTION 19

PREFACE 22

CHAPTER 1. **THE PLACE OF THE DRAGON IN CHINESE LIFE** 27

CHAPTER 2. **HOW THE DRAGON IDEA ORIGINATED** 36

CHAPTER 3. **THE VARIETIES OF DRAGONS** 41

CHAPTER 4. **WHAT DRAGONS REALLY LOOK LIKE** 49

CHAPTER 5. **PEOPLE WHO HAVE SEEN DRAGONS** 57

CHAPTER 6. **THE DRAGON IN WESTERN MYTHOLOGY** 65

CHAPTER 7. **QUAINT BELIEFS ABOUT THE DRAGON** 72

CHAPTER 8. **HOW DRAGONS CONTROL THE FORTUNES OF MEN** 78

CHAPTER 9. **THE HOLD OF THE DRAGON ON CHINA** 86

ILLUSTRATIONS

BRONZE DRAGON, KANGXI PERIOD 9

"DRAGON" IN CHINESE WRITING 13

DRAGON COLONNADE AT QUFU 18

THE "DRAGON DISK" 21

SURROUNDED BY DRAGONS 25

THE DRAGON THRONE OF THE EMPERORS 26

QIANLONG VASES 29

THE APPARITION OF THE TWO DRAGONS AND FIVE OLD MEN 32

THE HAN DYNASTY DRAGONS 33

THE PORCELAIN DRAGON SCREEN 35

THE YELLOW EMPEROR 37

THE DRAGON STAIRCASE 39

AN IMPERIAL DRAGON 40

TABLET OF CONFUCIUS 43

A DRAGON COLUMN 44

DRAGON GATEWAY 47

THE DRAGON STONE 48

GOLDEN CANTEEN 52

DRAGON-GUARDED ASTROLABE 53

A DRAGON-MOUNTED BELL 55

THE NINE DRAGON HANDSCROLLS 56

90-Year Anniversary Edition

A CLOUD DRAGON 60

CIRCULAR DRAGON EAVES TILE 63

THE HONGWU EMPEROR 64

A LIVING DRAGON 70

TWO PORCELAIN DRAGONS 71

THE "DRAGON SQUARE" 76

DEITIES RIDING DRAGONS ACROSS THE CLOUDS 77

EMPEROR TAIZU 79

EMPEROR KANGXI ON THE DRAGON THRONE 83

A DRAGON LANTERN 84

A DRAGON BOAT RACE IN FUZHOU 85

DRAGON AND PHOENIX MOTIF 88

DRAGON-TIGER MOUNTAIN, JIANGSI PROVINCE 89

THE GATEWAY TO THE DRAGON WELL 90

THE DRAGON TABLET 93

THE DRAGON FLAG 94

"DRAGON" IN CHINESE WRITING

"Dragon", pronounced *long* in Mandarin Chinese in writing: Oracle bone script, the oldest form of Chinese writing; Bronze script, as written on Chinese bronze artefacts from the Shang Dynasty to the Zhou Dynasty; Great seal script, an older variants of Seal Script; Seal Script, an ancient form of Chinese calligraphy; Traditional Chinese script.

EDITOR'S NOTE

REACHING THE TIME OF THE GREATEST TEST

Over the course of almost a century, China's government, geographical landscape, language and communication with the Western world has changed dramatically.

Although the author's studies on the Chinese dragon over 14 years remain valid, it has reached the time to test his prediction of the endurance of the widespread belief in this magnificent creature.

Under the rule of the Chinese Communist Party, Western science has permeated most, if not all, of China for over a generation. True to L. Newton Hayes's prediction, the historical and cultural beliefs of the Chinese people, particularly that of the younger generations, are therefore being tested.

The timing of the release of this edition—at the beginning of the Chinese Year of the Dragon, 2012—offers a catalyst to garner response to the author's prediction of 90 years ago.

THE AUTHOR'S HOPE IN CULTURAL ENDURANCE

It is unlikely that the author could have imagined the destruction bestowed upon the souls of the Chinese through the Cultural Revolution and subsequent persecutory campaigns against intellectuals, students, Falun Gong practitioners, minority groups and many others to eliminate faith in ancient Chinese traditions and beliefs.

For the younger generations, belief in the mythical and divine has all but been replaced with modern science and money drivers. Sightings, stories and reverence for the Chinese dragon have diminished.

Although written in all due seriousness of study, even myself, as a product of the current modern society, often marvel at the purity of belief in the author's subjects and the matter-of-fact representation of his findings presented in this book.

However, we can find inspiration from and admiration for the author and his hope in the endurance of his subject when he says,

> A belief that has gripped the nation for over forty centuries is not to be shaken even by an historic revolution... in relation to the ages which have passed, is little more than a ripple upon the surface of the sea of time.

CHANGES OVER 90 YEARS

Keeping true to the original text, this 90-year anniversary, and fourth edition, include the following changes:

- Footnotes with descriptions as well as updated place names and romanization of Chinese words to reflect the current Pinyin[1] system

---

[1] Pinyin is the official system used to transcribe Chinese characters into the Roman alphabet, developed by the Chinese Communist Party and approved in the 1950s. Previous romanization systems include the Wade-Giles system, which is

- New illustrations and photographs that were unavailable at the times of earlier editions

- Some original illustrations are not included due to poor quality, others have been edited for improved quality

- New cover design and layout formatting to reflect the fast-paced, scanning methods of reading in modern society

- New eBook format for digital distribution

- The use of Internet sources to source, update and verify information prior to publication

- Website www.TheChineseDragonBook.com and other online platforms to encourage interest in the creature and to aggregate any new dragon sightings or other information relevant to the content of this book

The formality of the original language has not been changed to remain true to the Western culture at the time of first publication.

And, to maintain the surprisingly pure beliefs and mythical atmosphere of the text, no additions of post-1911 Revolution political history, beyond the references in this Editor's Note, are included.

ILLUSTRATIONS OF ARTIFACTS

At the time of first publication, the artifacts and locations contained in the illustrations were still in existence in China. Although it is quite possible that a vast majority of them were destroyed during the Cultural Revolution by the Chinese Communist Party[2], the editor has not sought to visit China and verify their remains.

---

still common in history books, particularly those about Imperial China, including the first edition of this book in 1922.

[2] During the Cultural Revolution (1966-1976) led by then Chairman of the Chinese

For the benefit of the reader, let us hope that even if their physical existence was destroyed, the cultural value and purpose live on.

FUTURE EDITIONS

The recent renewal of interest in traditional Chinese culture, both in China and overseas, by native Chinese and non-Chinese alike, bring hope for a renewal of the great dragon.

Only time will tell if the author's prediction of endurance will be fulfilled and if future editions will speak of the dragon as fact or fiction.

Kay Rubacek

January 23, 2012

The first day of the Year of the Dragon, 2012, 90 years after the first publication of "The Chinese Dragon".

Communist Party, Mao Zedong, thousands of years of history were destroyed or later smuggled abroad for sale. Such destruction of historical sites, artifacts and archives is unmatched in history.

DRAGON COLONNADE AT QUFU

Ten stately stone columns stand in the Confucian Temple at Qufu, Shandong (formerly romanized as Chufu, Shantung). The pillars are monoliths of white marble, nearly twenty feet in height. These are decorated with huge dragons in deep relief. This is said to be the most perfect and most beautiful stone colonnade in China

INTRODUCTION

The subject of this little book is of general interest to people who are acquainted with things Chinese. The dragon has played a large part in Chinese thought through four thousand and more years, and even today, still fills an important place in Chinese life.

The dragon is one of the most common ornamental designs in China and one meets it wherever one goes in this country. However, in spite of the significance attached to the dragon very little[3] has ever been written concerning it in either Chinese or English.

Only a few general articles on this subject have been published in magazines, and the references to it in books are very brief. No independent study of the dragon in book form existed in either of these two languages prior to the publication of this book.

---

[3] Since publication of this book and the explosion of the information age and the Internet, there is a vastly increased range of resources available about the Chinese dragon. However, there are still very few well-researched publications written with the depth of knowledge of the author and using primary and secondary sources as included in this book, that offer an authority on the subject.

The author, L. Newton Hayes, is particularly fitted to undertake this piece of work. He was born in China and speaks the Chinese language as a native. Thus he has had the first-hand knowledge and the language to help him in his study.

At the time of writing this book, he had been studying on the subject of the dragon for fourteen years, during which time he traveled over more than one half the number of provinces of China. The study is therefore not the result of a few months' investigation, nor is it the product of research in only one city or province.

The author's acquaintance with the people and the language of China have made it possible for him to go to original sources and to study the subject from every angle.

Perhaps the last word on the Chinese dragon is not yet said, nevertheless it is safe to say that this treatise is as complete as our present knowledge will permit. This little volume should be of value to all who are interested in China.

This account of the dragon will not only be of value to foreigners, but it will also be such to Chinese. The author has made this study a hobby for many years and the result of his research is a splendid contribution to the literature on China.

It would be a good idea for more people to take up the study of other phases of Chinese life in the same way and thus help to interpret China to the West.

Fong F. Sec.

May 9, 1922.

THE "DRAGON DISK"

This exquisite design was the insignia worn by a prince of the imperial house of the Qing (formerly romanized as Ching) dynasty. The insignia of the prime minister was square like those of lower officials. Princes were distinguished by circular emblems. This dragon disk is eleven inches in diameter and is embroidered with gold and black.

PREFACE

THE AUTHOR'S FIRST MONTHS IN CHINA

In the spring of 1909 the writer had the honor of being a guest for a week in the summer home of Dr. W. A. P. Martin, near Beijing[4]. Many residents of the Capital during the decade preceding the Revolution[5], and for a number of years before that, knew "Pearl Grotto" and visited the venerable senior missionary of China, then lately retired from the Presidency of the Imperial Tongwen College[6].

Dr. Martin was a scholar of the old school and enjoyed few pursuits better than that of reviewing his remarkable memory of the classical writers. During the meals the old gentleman, then nearly eighty, would quote readily from Homer, Horace, and Virgil, and would ask his guest to translate the passages freely into English and to cite the books and chapters quoted.

[4] Formerly romanized as Peking.
[5] In October of 1911, a revolt against the Qing dynasty in southern China succeeded in ending the imperial system of and establishing the Republic of China.
[6] Formerly romanized as Tung Wen, the college was a government school for teaching Western languages, founded during the late Qing dynasty.

After a few days in this uncomfortable situation the guest began to cast about for some means of relief. At that time he had been in the country but a few months, and was just beginning a general study of Chinese art. The dragon, among other objects of interest, particularly attracted his attention.

LITTLE DRAGON KNOWLEDGE AMONG THE EXPERTS

It occurred to him to ask Dr. Martin some questions about this creature whose form was so popular with the Chinese. Accordingly a carefully prepared list of six or seven questions about the dragon was launched one morning across the breakfast table before the attack of Greek and Latin began.

The first question met with a noncommittal reply, the second fared little better, and so on to the end. Then Dr. Martin admitted that this was one of the subjects about which he knew very little. He was, however, very warm in his desire to help find answers to these questions, and he referred his guest to his personal friend, Sir Robert Hart, the Inspector General of the Imperial Customs, who had also lived fifty years in China.

Unfortunately Sir Robert's replies were as vague as those of the retired Professor. The questions which were asked of these two eminent Sinologues were also submitted to several other British and Americans in Beijing, and later to many Chinese, but with similar results.

THE SEARCH FOR ORIGINAL SOURCES

It soon became evident that if the searcher for light on "Things Chinese" were to learn much about this creature which had challenged his attention, he must look it up from original sources. He was later convinced of this fact when he found it impossible to secure any satisfactory information from books published in English.

A COMMITMENT TO COMPLETE A STUDY

He then resolved that before he himself was fifteen years in the country he would have answers to the seven questions which he had asked of his friends in Beijing.

The contents of this publication are the results of a study made in ten provinces of China over a period of fourteen years.

UPON COMPLETION OF THE WORK

While this volume is not offered as the final word upon this subject, it probably represents the most exhaustive study thus far given to the Chinese dragon.

This book is not intended primarily for sinologists and it contains no Chinese characters. The volume is written for the average reader, who in his study of things Chinese, has little time to go to original sources. Most people do not wish to be burdened with long quotations to prove abstract hypotheses or to have Chinese characters inserted in the text repeatedly to break the sequence.

If later interest in this subject justifies it, a larger work will be attempted and a more detailed presentation of the material thus far collected will be made.

The writer's purpose in this book has been to make as clear a statement of the subject as could be done within the compass of a small book, without introducing unnecessary material. If he has succeeded in this endeavor, he will be more than gratified.

SURROUNDED BY DRAGONS

This palace portrait was a prized possession of the Manchu emperors. Yung Cheng, the son of Kangxi, is here shown upon the throne, which he ascended in 1723. Countless dragons entertain themselves upon his costly robes of state and writhe and wreathe themselves in the lattice structure of his imperial throne.

THE DRAGON THRONE OF THE EMPERORS

This massive structure, surmounted by countless dragons, stands in the Imperial Palace in Peking. From the dragon throne issued the decrees which, before the republic, controlled the destinies of one quarter of the human race.

CHAPTER ONE:
THE PLACE OF THE DRAGON IN CHINESE LIFE

THERE ARE REAL DRAGONS LIVING IN CHINA TODAY

These are not the horrible monsters that some have imagined them to be. They are friendly creatures highly revered by all the people.

They possess marvelous powers and they occasionally permit themselves to be seen by mortal eyes. Such is the belief of at least seven out of every ten Chinese.

The popular belief in the dragon is so deeply rooted and so widespread that it is advisable for one to secure an accurate knowledge of the Chinese idea of the venerated saurian[7] if he desires to gain a truly sympathetic understanding of this remarkable people.

DRAGONS INFLUENCE MANY ASPECTS OF CHINESE LIFE

---

[7] Any of the various reptiles of the suborder, Sauria, which included the lizards and in former classifications, also the crocodiles and dinosaurs.

Nearly every phase of Chinese life bears evidence of the influence of this unique member of the animal kingdom. Particularly is this true in the realms of their art, literature, folklore, zoology, history, and religion.

CHINESE ART

Chinese art employs dragon designs in endless variety. The graceful lines of its symmetrically proportioned body are found in every part of the country painted upon silks and porcelain, woven into brocades, carved on wood, embroidered upon satin, cast in bronze, and chiseled upon marble.

It is the most characteristically Chinese of the many Oriental designs which are so attractive to Western students of art.

CHINESE LITERATURE

The literature of the country abounds in references to this marvelous creature as one may readily discover by even a cursory study of its books of history, poetry, letters, medicine, and fiction.

CHINESE FOLKLORE

Chinese folklore is replete with countless entertaining stories of the wonderful feats of this great animal, while an infinite number of proverbs and old folks' sayings bear their testimony to the almost universal belief in its existence.

QIANLONG VASES

These two dainty porcelain vases of the Qianlong (formerly romanized as Chien Lung) period were "burned" a little over three hundred years ago. The paws of the dragon each contain five claws. Creamy clouds and red flames of fire fill in the background, while conventional green waves decorate the base.

CHINESE ZOOLOGY AND NATURAL HISTORY

Popular zoology places the dragon next to man, at the head of the list of all living creatures, thus occupying the position of the lion or tiger in our Western classification.

Strictly speaking, Chinese natural history gives the dragon the rank of king only of scale-covered animals or creatures which live in the sea; the two fabulous creatures, the *qilin*[8] and the Phoenix respectively, have first place above all beasts and other animals which live upon the earth, and all birds and other creatures which fly in the air. But because the dragon is equally at home in the air and on the earth, as well as in the sea, it has been ranked as the ruler of all created life below man.

CHINESE GEOMANCY

Chinese geomancy for ages has looked to the dragon as a means of determining the fates and fortunes of the "Sons of Han", or Chinese people. Until very recently comparatively few Chinese would build a house or bury a corpse without first consulting a geomancer, who would, in one way or another, refer to its probable influence upon his action. It is, moreover, a generally accepted belief that every twelfth hour, day, month, and year of the lunar calendar are under the dragon's dominating control.

HISTORICAL CONNECTIONS

Chinese history records scores of appearances of the king of beasts through the four thousand or more years since the age of the three mythical ruler[9]. Appearances of the dragon are connected with the stories of many prominent characters of China's past.

---

[8] The Qilin, formerly romanized as Chi Ling, is a mythical guardian described as having a dragon head, lion body and scales.
[9] The Three Mythical Rulers, also known as the Three Sovereigns or the Three August Ones are cultural heroes from ancient China, said to be exemplary sages or god-kings who possessed great moral character and used their powers to improve

Perhaps the most noteworthy reference is one which states that two dragons as guards of honor visited the home of Confucius on the day that great sage was born. These frequent references to the dragon are considered, for the most part, by the majority of Chinese scholars quite as authentic as the statements about the famous worthies themselves.

CHINESE RELIGION

Chinese religion places the dragon in the calendar of its deities as the God of Rain and Ruler of Rivers, Lakes, and Seas. As such it has been worshiped for centuries. There are probably very few cities of any size in the whole country, which, at least until the recent revolution, were without a temple or shrine to the dragon king.

This deity was worshipped on the first and fifteenth of every month.

WESTERN MISCONCEPTIONS

In the opinion of the writer, dwellers in other lands commonly think of the dragon in much the same light as they think of the centaurs, of Geryon or the Minotaur of Grecian fables: a strange mythical creature merely the product of human fancy. It is also probable that most of them think that the majority of Chinese consider it in the same way, but this is a mistaken conception.

---

the lives of their people.

THE APPARITION OF THE TWO DRAGONS AND FIVE OLD MEN

The evening when Confucius was born, two dragons encircled the house. In the great court of honor the five old men, or the spirits of the five planets, Venus, Jupiter, Mercury, Mars and Saturn, were seen to descend. (Image from *Researches into Chinese Superstitions* by Henry Dore, S.J., 1938)

THE HAN DYNASTY DRAGONS

The brick upon which these dragons are molded was baked over two thousand years ago. It was dug up recently near Kaifeng, in Henan (formerly romanized as Honan) province, one of the Seven Ancient Capitals of China.

When two dragons appear in art they usually face each other. On this ancient brick the reverse is true. The circle through which these animals have wound themselves has become, in modern art, a disk. Most dragons are portrayed gazing intently at the disk, which is usually described as the sun. The simplicity of these dragons is very marked in contrast to the elaborate designs of the present day.

BELIEF BEYOND MYTHOLOGY

It may be considered a very conservative estimate to state that at least three hundred and sixty million Chinese believe in the actual existence of dragons as firmly as other peoples believe that there are such animals as tigers roaming in the jungles of Bengal and such monsters as walruses wandering over the icy stretches which border the arctic circle, though they themselves may never have set foot upon the shores of India nor have crossed the Arctic Sea.

LOCAL STUDY

Quite recently the writer made a localized study of the universality of the belief in dragons. One hundred representative Chinese of different ages and walks in life in an important city were asked the following questions:

> Do you believe in the present existence of the dragon? And what percentage of the people of China do you think hold this belief?

Eighty-two of the one hundred answered the first question in the affirmative.

Regarding the universality of the belief in the dragon these men estimated that at least 86.6 per cent of their fellow nationals believe in its existence.

The above study bore out very accurately the writer's estimate of the extent of the popular belief in the dragon. His judgment was based upon questions asked many scores of Chinese in ten different provinces of the country through a period of fourteen years.

THE PORCELAIN DRAGON SCREEN

Nine huge dragons of many colors frolic upon this imperial screen. It is approximately one hundred feet long and twenty feet high. This impressive structure, faced with porcelain tiles of the finest texture, stood on the edge of the "North Sea," within the walls of the Imperial Palace in Beijing.

CHAPTER TWO:
HOW THE DRAGON IDEA ORIGINATED

ANCIENT ZOOLOGICAL ORIGINS

The elaborate conception of the dragon, which we find today in Chinese art and literature, is undoubtedly a very different animal from the one, which was responsible for the origin of the dragon idea.

The fabled sea serpent, the alligator, the salamander, and the boa constrictor have each been regarded as the prototype of this unique creature.

It is far more likely, however, that some ancient saurian, or reptile, was the true source from which the dragon idea has sprung. Back in the dawn of history some early member of the human race may have met with one of these monstrous creatures which paleontologists tell us were, in some period of their development, equally at home on land and in the sea, and because of its gigantic size and marvelous powers attributed to it a supernatural origin.

In later ages, even the unearthed skeleton of one of these monsters might have been sufficient to have led to the inception of the story. If this theory is correct it is easy to understand how through succeeding ages the belief could have grown and how superstition and coincidence would have done their share to elaborate from the early monster the marvelous creature of the present day.

According to the theory advanced above, the writer believes that the most probable prototype of the dragon is the Brontosaurus of the Mesozoic age, although the present conception of the dragon may easily have sprung from such other prehistoric animals.

Skeletons of these giants of the saurian family and pictures of the reconstructed animals indicate a striking resemblance to the graceful creatures that dominate the art of China.

THE FIRST APPEARANCE IN CHINA

The first appearance of the true dragon, according to the records of what is considered to be authentic Chinese history, occurred some forty-six centuries ago during the reign of the great historical figure and cultural hero, Huang Di, or the Yellow Emperor, who is often regarded as the initiator of Chinese civilization.

We are told that after this personage had reigned one hundred and eleven years a large dragon appeared and took him to heaven upon his back. Since that

THE YELLOW EMPEROR

day dragons have been seen in every dynasty and by hundreds of witnesses, as Chinese history abundantly attests.

THE AUSPICIOUSNESS OF SIGHTING A DRAGON

Dragon appearances were considered auspicious, and brought good fortune for the affairs of state.

In support of this belief, it is interesting to note that when the late President Yuan Shikai[10] was trying to make himself emperor his friends made at least one attempt to unearth what were supposed to be the bones of a dragon.

This was done in order that the superstitious among his countrymen might be led to feel that his desire to reestablish the empire was according to the law of heaven.

For centuries it was the custom for anyone who saw a dragon, either himself or through the magistrate of the district in which he lived, immediately to announce the fact to the emperor. In early days history was often counted from the appearance of a particular dragon.

A popular fable relates that Yu Wang was able to end the great flood 2297 BC only after he had succeeded in capturing the dragon, who was said to be responsible for the deluge. The animal was chained in heavy irons and imprisoned, after which the flood subsided.

Ever since that time all dragons, we are told, have trembled at the memory of the only man who ever conquered their kind.

---

[10] The second President of the Republic of China, after Sun Yatsen, who was in power at the time of first publication of this book.

THE DRAGON STAIRCASE

In most Confucian and imperial temples the center of the path that leads from the temple entrance to the sacred shrine is known as the spirit way. Where this route leads up a staircase, one usually finds not steps but a large inclined stone on which are carved one or more dragons. At the hour of worship the spirit of the one who is honored, travels, we are told, over this course. The dragon monolith shown in this photograph leads up to the smallest, the central one, of the three altars at the Temple of Heaven in Beijing.

AN IMPERIAL DRAGON

This lifelike creature, symbolic of imperial power, adorns one of the walls within the palace ground of Beijing. Here, as in most representations, the dragon is shown gazing longingly at the flaming sun. He desires, we are told, not so much to seize the heavenly body as to learn the secret of its brilliance, so that it may add to his own glory.

CHAPTER THREE:
THE VARIETIES OF DRAGONS

DRAGON SPECIES

To the majority of people the word "dragon" denotes one animal only. There are, however, at least eight species of animals, which bear this name. They all belong to the genus dragon, *Long*[11], but each has one or more characteristics, which differentiates it from the others.

For example, the *Li Long*, or *Chih Long*, as it is also named, has and is the only species that possesses wings. It is, however, but one of these species, the *Shen Long*[12], which will be considered at this time. Of the eight varieties this is the one best known. The others may be dismissed with a word.

Dr. Williams, in his "Middle Kingdom,"[13] mentions only three varieties and says that these are respectively dragons of the sky, of

---

[11] Formerly romanized as Lung.
[12] Literally translates to "spirit dragon"
[13] "The Middle Kingdom, A survey of the geography, government, literature, social

the sea, and of marshes. However, it seems that the Chinese are not generally accustomed to make such a classification. They rather consider that the one species, Shen Long, controls and operates in all of these three spheres. Most of the other varieties are minor creatures, which are practically unknown and have slight bearing upon this study.

THE DRAGON KING

The one exception to the abovementioned rule is the *Long Wang*, or dragon king. This species differs from the others in that its members possess a dragon's head upon a human body. By some this dragon is said to answer to Neptune in Western mythology.

Each ocean has a dragon king. The members of this species differ from those of the one in which we are the most interested in that dragon kings rarely grow old and never die. The remaining varieties are all quite secondary and practically never appear in any form of art. These are mentioned only occasionally in Chinese literature.

This book will therefore be confined to an account of the Shen Long, or spirit dragon, the real dragon, the dragon that has held China in its spell since the days of Yao and Shun.[14]

---

life, arts and history, of The Chinese Empire and Its Inhabitants," by S. Wells Williams, Professor of the Chinese language and literature at Yale College, revised edition 1907.

[14] Legendary Chinese rulers. Shun served as a Minister to Emperor Yao before being appointed by Yao as his successor to the throne.

TABLET OF CONFUCIUS

This red lacquer tablet, inscribed with eight characters in gold, stood in the shrine of a temple in Hangzhou, Zhejiang province. The inscription may be freely translated, "The Sacred Tablet of Our Revered Teacher Confucius."

The tablet is approximately four feet high and one foot wide. Nine dragons play hide and seek in the framework that borders the edge of the inscription. Two larger dragons twine themselves about the slender pillars before the shrine. These serve as guards of honor. These two creatures symbolize the two dragons which, history says, encircled the home of Confucius when the sage was born. Similar tablets were found in all temples to Confucius throughout China.

A DRAGON COLUMN

This remarkable monolith stood near the entrance to the famous Ming Tombs, thirty miles north of Beijing. A huge dragon, surrounded by clouds, wraps itself closely about the tall shaft. There were two of these columns at the Ming Tombs, one on either side of the Spirit Road. The five-clawed dragons symbolize the imperial nature of the extensive cemetery where were buried thirteen emperors, each in his massive mausoleum.

THE TWO KINDS OF TRUE DRAGONS

All true dragons are of two kinds: those that are such by birth and those that become dragons by transformation from fish of the carp species.

TRANSFORMED AT THE "DRAGON'S GATE"

The transformed variety become dragons by leaping up the waters of a certain cataract upon a western mountain stream. Large numbers of carp swim once each year, we learn, to this waterfall known as the "Dragon's Gate." Here under the cataract they flounder about, jumping and springing up out of the swirling waters; a few of them succeed in getting over the falls to the higher waters above. Those that are successful in this effort become dragons.

After the story of this strange occurrence became known to the public, it was incorporated into the life of the people in a popular saying, and scholars who succeeded in passing the great triennial literary examinations were said to have "passed the Dragon Gate." The use of this figure was doubtless to illustrate the difficulty of passing the examinations, for it implied that it was as difficult a task for a man to succeed at these examinations as it was for the carp to leap up over the falls.

This figure has, in addition, the happy inference that even as the carp, an ordinary fish, might become a mighty dragon, just so by this supreme effort a scholar might become a master of arts, thus placing the value of the transformation on a very high scale.

LAZY DRAGONS

One ancient authority tells us that there is a class of these great lizards that are known as "lazy dragons." These do not like to exert themselves in the task of directing clouds that carry rain over the surface of the earth.

They sometimes make themselves small in size, drop to the surface of the earth and hide in trees, under roofs of houses, and even in the clothing of unsuspecting countrymen.

The Thunder God, learning of the desertion from their posts of duty sends his messengers to search for them and when he discovers their location, kills them with thunderbolts, like the Greek God Zeus, during an electric storm.

This explains to many an unsophisticated man the frequent destruction of life and property during thunderstorms. A descriptive phrase that in some parts of the country is often hurled at lazy people is *Lan Long* or " lazy dragon."

DRAGON GATEWAY

Within the main entrance to Nanking's Examination Hall, where the Master's Degree was earned, stood a long "spirit wall." Upon the front of this structure was painted a dragon gate, beneath which was shown a carp changing into a dragon. A Bachelor of Arts, according to China's ancient system of education, upon becoming a Master, was congratulated by his friends as having passed through the "Dragon Gate." The implication was that it was as difficult for a Bachelor of Arts to become a Master as for a carp to be transformed into a dragon.

THE DRAGON STONE

In the city of Kaifeng, Hunan province, the first capital of the Song emperors, is a sacred building known as the "Dragon Pavilion." Within this structure, which stands high above most of the buildings of the city, is a large basaltic stone known as the "Dragon Throne." This is cut in the form of a cube of about six feet in each dimension and rests under the shrine of the Emperor.

Nine hundred years ago the Song emperors doubtlessly placed their lacquered thrones upon its upper surface. In order to protect it from vandal hands, the historic stone was incased within wooden walls, which form a cavelike room about it. Fourteen dragons in deep relief surround the outer edge: five on the front and back faces, and two on either end.

Visitors must use candles in order to see at all in the inky darkness. Because of the narrow quarters no photograph can be taken. This drawing by a Kaifeng artist was made under the greatest difficulties and is probably the first reproduction ever attempted.

CHAPTER FOUR:
WHAT DRAGONS REALLY LOOK LIKE

WHO REALLY KNOWS?

Comparatively few Chinese of the older generation seem to question the existence of dragons or to doubt the marvelous powers usually attributed to them. In view of this fact it is surprising to find how ignorant is the average person who holds this belief when asked to give an accurate description of the great creature.

Perhaps this is not strange, however, when we remember that there are apparently no books that give any complete account of the dragon.

The innumerable references to it in Chinese literature largely deal with the dragon's performances and say little about his appearance.

In order to make a satisfactory study of the dragon one must, therefore, follow a tedious process of collecting, eliminating, and coordinating a multitude of stories, proverbs, and incidents from history, and make a careful study of selected pictures and carvings, and if possible secure interviews with those who profess to have seen the great king of the animal creation.

One writer, who is anxious to make intelligible to the average person the accepted representation of the king of all created life below man, describes the dragon in terms of animals with many of which we are quite familiar. He says that it has:

> ...the head of a camel, the horns of a deer, the ears of a cow, the neck of a snake, the body of a fish, the scales of a carp, the claws of an eagle, the eyes of a devil, and the paws of a tiger.

THREE BODY SECTIONS OF EQUAL LENGTH

The bodies of all dragons, we are informed, are symmetrically divided into three sections of equal length, these divisions being from the point of the nose to the shoulders, from the shoulders to the thighs, and from the thighs to the tip of the tail.

A CHANGEABLE LENGTH

The "Shoh Wen," a book written during the Tang dynasty, says that the dragon has the following marvelous powers:

> It may cause itself to become visible or invisible at will, and it can become long or short, and coarse or fine, at its own good pleasure.

This wonderful versatility of course, makes it difficult for us to find any recorded statement of the maximum length of this creature, since there is no limit set for its expansion.

Another book of the Tang dynasty helps out a little, however, when it describes a certain dragon, which was found dead, as having been over one hundred feet long, while other accounts lead us to believe that the dragon at times assumes a size several miles in length. The smallest size of which any statement has been found was the length of a silkworm.

FIVE COLORS

In color, dragons are differentiated as being red, yellow, blue, white, or black.

During the Manchu Dynasty, yellow was the imperial color, and the yellow or golden dragon was designated the imperial dragon. In the preceding dynasty, the Ming dynasty, when red was the national color, it is believed that the red dragon was proclaimed, by decree of the emperor, the official dragon of the empire.

FOUR OR FIVE CLAWS

Every careful observer in the Far East has noticed a difference in the number of claws in the pictures of dragons—some possessing three, others four, and still others five claws. The smallest number is found on the dragons of Japanese art.

Ordinarily, Chinese dragons have four claws, while those of five were recognized as imperial dragons. The two types of Chinese dragons, with these slight variations, are, however, one and the same species, and are identical in every other respect.

An attempt has been made to prove that the variation of claws from three through four to five is a historic development, but we can find no conclusive proof to substantiate this theory.

It is possible that the ancient dragon designs of China have only three claws on each foot. Japan borrowed her art from China, and it is not unlikely that at the period when she borrowed this design the Chinese dragon was represented with only three claws.

GOLDEN CANTEEN

A golden canteen decorated with a five-clawed imperial dragon from the Ming Dynasty. (Image by PericlesOfAthen, Wikimedia Commons)

DRAGON-GUARDED ASTROLABE

This exquisitely wrought bronze instrument for measuring the position of the stars was on display in Beijing. It stood at the foot of the ramp leading to the Imperial Observatory. Four hundred years ago the Jesuit astronomer Veribest had this, and a score of other magnificent instruments, cast for the Emperor Kangxi. Most of these great pieces are surmounted or protected by dragons of the finest workmanship.

EIGHTY-ONE SCALES IN EACH SERIES

It is said of the carp that it always has exactly thirty-six scales in each row, leading from its head to its tail. After the same manner, dragons are described as possessing eighty-one scales in each series.

NINE SONS

The true dragon has nine[15] sons. Each is different in appearance from the other and each possesses his own peculiar characteristics.

These children of the dragon are the variants in appearance from the general line which we are accustomed to look for in the dragon, and which we often see in carvings and architecture.

The dragon heads on bells, on the peak tiles of temples and palaces, on sword hilts, on monuments, and in similar places are representations of the progeny of the God of Rain and do not portray that god himself.

---

[15] Editor's Note: In Chinese culture, the number nine is considered an auspicious number and is very much connected with Chinese dragons.

A DRAGON-MOUNTED BELL

Three dragons unite themselves to form the structure from which hangs this graceful bell. The frame is of redwood from southern China and, like much of the carvings from the city of Fuzhou, it is richly inlaid with silver. A fourth dragon coils over the surface of the bell. Two dragon-like heads unite to form the loop by which the bell is hung. These represent one variety of the nine sons of the king of the animal world.

THE NINE DRAGON HANDSCROLLS

One of the dragons from *The Nine Dragons* handscroll painted by the Song-Dynasty Chinese artist Chen Rong with ink and some red on paper. The entire scroll is 18.2 x 431.7 inches (46.3 x 1096.4 cm).

CHAPTER FIVE:
PEOPLE WHO HAVE SEEN DRAGONS

DRAGON SIGHTINGS

In spite of the fact that modern zoology has never included in the pages of its textbooks descriptions and pictures of the dragon as a creature of reality, yet there are men in China today who claim to have seen these animals, some of which have been described very accurately.

The writer has had the pleasure of conversing with several Chinese who assert that they have seen the dragon at close range. He has also secured, at secondhand, information from others who are said to have looked upon this most marvelous of creatures.

All of the men whom the writer interviewed were of sound mind and were accredited by their acquaintances with being men of reliable character. There is no reason to believe that any one of them were intoxicated or under the power of hallucination at the time they witnessed the creatures of their description.

FALLEN TO EARTH

A teacher in a Tianjin[16] school related that he once saw a dragon in his native province, Shandong[17]. The animal had been killed, so it was believed, by the order of heaven, as a punishment for some misdeed, and had fallen to the earth, where it lay as the center of attraction for hundreds of people who came in crowds from that whole countryside. Its appearance was identical with that of the popular pictures with which we are familiar.

FIFTEEN-FOOT DRAGON

A school servant, who was also a native of Shandong, and whose home was near the sea, declared that he once saw a dragon. He told the writer that it was about fifteen feet long and that it fell to the earth during a severe rainstorm. It, too, attracted a large crowd of spectators.

Although this man was unable to give very satisfactory details, his unusual earnestness and apparent sincerity were convincing evidence that he had really seen a monster of a remarkable type.

FIFTY-FOOT DRAGON

A third person, an elderly gentleman, who is a teacher of classics in one of the schools of Nanjing[18], informed the writer that when he was a young man a dragon fell one night from the sky and lay for twenty-four hours near his home.

The country folk respectfully covered it with matting, but he managed to raise the covering and saw its great cow-like head, its four legs, and its scale-covered body. It was about fifty feet long and blue in color.

---

[16] Formerly romanized as Tientsin. A city in northern China.
[17] Formerly romanized as Shantung. A province on the eastern coast of China.
[18] Formerly romanized as Nanking or Nan-ching. The capital of Jiansu province.

As in the other two cases, this dragon disappeared from the earth during a heavy storm. It was generally believed that it came to life again and was taken up into the heavens upon a cloud, which formed beneath its body.

THE CLOUD DRAGON

The artist who drew the picture of the cloud dragon recounted that, during the thirty-fourth year of the Emperor Guangxu[19], while he himself was on his way to Beijing[20] to receive the seals of a district magistrate, he came across a dragon lying upon the banks of the Yellow River in Shandong province.

It was blue in color and was several tens of feet in length. The whole air was filled with a very offensive salt sea odor, and out of respect for the creature, which was supposed to have fallen from heaven, the crowd of people that stood around was busily engaged in sprinkling water upon its body.

The head resembled that of a cow and the artist said that except for the long eyebrows the picture of the cloud dragon represented very faithfully what he actually saw.

THREE DRAGONS CROSSING THE MOUNTAINS

Another Chinese has related that a business partner of his, while on a journey up the Yangtze River, saw three dragons crossing a mountain range near the shore.

Every person on board was spellbound as they watched the three monsters—one yellow, another white, and the third blue—as they majestically made their way with great undulating strides up the mountain side.

---

[19] Formerly romanized as Kuang Hsu. The eleventh emperor of the Qing Dynasty.
[20] Formerly romanized as Peking. Now the capital of the People's Republic of China, the city has been at the heart of China's history for centuries.

A CLOUD DRAGON

One of the men who claimed to have seen a living dragon was by profession an artist. This medallion was drawn by him: "Except for the whiskers, this painting represents what I saw when a young man in Shantung province."

The cloud dragon is a favorite theme of artists. Dragons are supposed to travel about upon the clouds. It is a common belief, and one which was held also by Confucius, that clouds spring from dragons. An ancient and well-known saying declares: "Clouds come from dragons and wind from tigers."

The dragons passed by so near the boat that the observers saw every detail of their heads and the lace-like scales of their bodies. The boat was respectfully stopped in mid-river, and only when the dragons had disappeared over the ridge did the boatmen resume their task at the oars.

FOG AND CLOUD SIGHTINGS

Various stories have come to the writer, of dragons that have been seen either riding upon banks of fog or dangling from passing clouds during great windstorms or rainstorms. Invariably these have been described as having scale-covered bodies.

One reasonable explanation for the suspended dragons may be found in insipient tornadoes and water spouts which never reach the ground.

ALTERNATIVE EXPLANATIONS

There seems, however, to be no explanation for the dragon visits described by the five observers, unless it be that strange monsters of the deep either crawled up out of the river and lay on the bank, in a dormant state, or were sucked up by ocean- or river-water spouts, and when the columns of water broke over the land the creatures were dropped far from their natural habitat.

Two difficulties at once present themselves to combat this hypothesis. The first of these is the improbability that there are such creatures in existence, and the second difficulty lies in the strangeness of their disappearance after coming to the earth.

As a possible explanation of the first difficulty, we wish to ask whether it is not possible that there are still existing in the depths of the sea and in great rivers curious reptiles and strange monsters such as no human beings now living have ever seen, the descendants of the mighty saurians which lived upon the earth long ages ago, and which geologists tell us later entered the sea, making that their more secretive habitat?

As an explanation for the disappearance of the dragon in these three instances the writer notes two facts: the dragons in each case were seen on the banks of great rivers and in each case disappeared after a heavy rain.

Might it not have been that the monsters were in reality not dead but only unconscious, and that the heavy flood washed the creatures back into the river whence they were carried out to sea?

CIRCULAR DRAGON EAVES TILE

This tile was found in the debris near the Ming Tomb of Nanjing. The body of the Hongwu Emperor, also known as Chu Yuan Chang, the founder of the Ming dynasty and the only emperor buried in the imperial cemetery east of Nanjing, was buried about 1399. This tile is of dark yellow porcelain, eight inches in diameter. It is probably six hundred years old.

THE HONGWU EMPEROR

Official court painting of the Hongwu Emperor, the founder of the Ming dynasty, with decorative dragons on his robe.

CHAPTER SIX:
THE DRAGON IN WESTERN MYTHOLOGY

WESTERN REFERENCES

The dragon is not a conception of the Chinese mind alone. It also occupies a prominent place in the legends and literature of most of the countries of Europe.

Cicero in his "de Divinatione"[21], Euripides in his "Philostratus"[22], and Homer in the "Iliad"[23] all mention a dragon.

The Bible, in twenty-two references in the Old Testament and thirteen instances in the New, refers to the dragon either allegorically or as a real animal; however, in many of these passages, especially in the Old Testament, the word "dragon" is an unfortunate rendition, for in several places the writers of the Scriptures very evidently had the conception of an animal that was in all probability the modern jackal.

---

[21] Book II, line 30
[22] Book I, line 2
[23] Book II, line 309

The myths and legends of Europe have preserved for us numerous dragon stories with which we are more or less familiar. Among others are the tale of Perseus, who rescued Andromeda from a dragon; the story of St. George and the Dragon; the account of Sigfried, who killed a dragon at Worms; and the story of Beowulf, who in the early days of history's dawn dispatched a dragon after slaying Grendel.

King Arthur, who was spoken of as the "dread Pendragon," is described by Tennyson, in his "Idylls of the King," as sitting upon a veritable dragon throne which would vie in splendor with that of China's Manchu emperors.

The vivid imagination of the poet laureate gives us this picture:

> To his crown the golden dragon clung
>
> And down his robe the dragon writhed in gold
>
> And from the carven work behind him crept
>
> Two dragons gilded, sloping down to make
>
> Arms to his chair, while all the rest of them
>
> Through knots and loops and folds innumerable.
>
> Fled ever through the woodwork till they found
>
> The new design wherein they lost themselves.

Many coast and river cities of England, France, Italy, and Egypt still proudly recount their local legends of cruel dragons which were slain, after battles royal, upon near-by rivers or in adjacent seas.

We may read of the Green Dragon of Mordiford, the Dragon of Norwich, the Great Dragon of Pittempton, the Dragon of Naples, the Dragon of Aries, the Dragon of Lyons, the Dragon of Marseilles, Sebec, the Dragon of the Nile, and many more. These stories are proudly treasured as the sacred traditions of their respective cities and countries.

FEW POINTS OF SIMILARITY

The Chinese conception of the dragon presents a very different creature from that of the nations bordering on the Mediterranean and the Atlantic. It is true that there are a few points of similarity, but there is only one to which we shall call attention at this time; that is regarding its keenness of eyesight.

EXCELLENT EYESIGHT

Both types of dragons are endowed with marvelous vision.

The Chinese dragon is deaf and it is explained that its eyes, through natural compensation, have attained an extraordinary power. His vision is so keen that he can easily distinguish a blade of grass one hundred *li*[24] away.

In this connection it is interesting to recall that the English word "dragon" is derived from the Greek "drakon", which means "to gaze" or "to see," and the classics more than once refer to the animal as "sharpsighted."

THREE SIGNIFICANT DIFFERENCES

We do not know who first attached the English name "dragon" to the Chinese conception "long[25]," but it is hardly fair to the Oriental ruler of the sea to be branded with the stigma that accompanies the English designation.

---

[24] A traditional Chinese unit of distance previously without a fixed measure. The modern standardized li is 500 meters or half a kilometre.
[25] Formerly romanized as and referred to in previous editions of this book as *lung*.

A misconception of the use of the word "dragon" had caused the speakers to confuse the evil monster mentioned in the book of Revelation with the animal so highly revered by the Chinese.

The dragon of the Chinese differs from the generally accepted Western idea in three striking particulars: in appearance, in disposition, and in the regard in which it is held.

APPEARANCE

In appearance, the European conception varies but slightly from the creature which was its probable prototype, save for the addition of a pair of wings.

The Chinese species is developed to a higher degree. The Western species has a more massive head from which protrude two branching horns.

The Chinese, with the single exception of the Chih Long, or Li Long, has no wings but travels from place to place upon the clouds.

DISPOSITION

A still greater difference between the two varieties exists in the matter of disposition. The European dragon is usually portrayed as a cruel monster, the personification of all that is evil, and the enemy of man.

Christian art represents it as opposed to law, harmony, and progress and symbolic of sin and paganism. In this allegorical sense it is painted in struggles with St. George, St. Michael, and St. Sylvester, who personified Christianity and enlightenment. Saints and martyrs are pictured in the process of crushing the dragon beneath their feet.

The Chinese dragon, on the other hand, is in this respect very nearly its antithesis. It is a beneficent creature, a friend to man. It brings the rain that produces the crops that in turn supply his food.

ESTEEM

The third point of distinction between the two dragons lies in the esteem in which it is held. The Western species was a horrible, loathsome creature, shunned and dreaded by all mortals, while the Asiatic dragon is held in reverence and even worshiped by the Chinese.

This creature is in fact so highly revered that one of the most sacred titles that was bestowed upon the emperors was "The True Dragon."

A LIVING DRAGON

Most representations of the dragon indicate peaceful, passive creatures. The artist who designed this dragon for the garden of the emperors at Beijing was a master of his art. This graceful creature fairly throbs with life, and we almost hold our breath as we look with the expectation that it will detach itself from the mural background and launch out into space. It is a living thing, and we feel that in another moment it will jerk back its head and rise to disappear before our very eyes.

TWO PORCELAIN DRAGONS

Of the nine huge saurians that play in the emerald waves beneath the pale blue sky on the imperial screen at Beijing, no two assume the same attitude. Leaping, springing, and lunging, each is struggling to reach the sun disk, which lies just out of reach before its face.

CHAPTER SEVEN:
QUAINT BELIEFS ABOUT THE DRAGON

DRAGON WHISKERS

According to a book of the Yuan dynasty,

> The whiskers of the dragon are three feet long and purple in color. If dragon whiskers are mounted upon a crystal handle like a horsehair whip and are placed in a room at night, flies and mosquitoes will not enter.

We are further informed,

> ...if this instrument is swished through the air it will make such a noise that chickens, dogs, cows, and horses on hearing it will try to hide. If dragon whiskers are placed in deep water, all scale-covered animals will swim immediately to the spot, thinking that their master, the dragon, is there.

BODY FIRE

A strange fire plays about the body of the dragon. This differs from the fire with which we are familiar in that it blazes brightly when brought into contact with water. If, however, terrestrial fire touches the dragon flames, the latter will immediately be extinguished.

MOISTURE AND MOTION

As long as the dragon has moisture in the form of water or clouds surrounding its body, it retains its marvelous powers of motion and of mutability, but when this moisture dries up, the dragon becomes powerless and dies.

DRAGON BLOOD

It is said that the blood of some dragons is red; of others, black. Rubies are often supposed to be petrified drops of the red variety.

BONE CHANGES

We are informed of the remarkable fact that dragons change their bones periodically and as regularly as snakes shed their skins and deer their horns.

Dragon bones are supposed to be buried in many high mountains, and their presence has much to do with the determination of Feng Shui.

Lofty peaks that are frequently tipped with clouds or enveloped in mist are believed to contain the bones of some great dragon which attract to themselves the moisture of the passing clouds.

PURPLE SALIVA

The saliva of the dragon, we are told, is purple in color, and is considered the most fragrant of all perfumes. It is said to be used in the manufacture of a very valuable incense. "Dragon's saliva incense" was formerly sent as a tribute to the emperor by one of the western provinces.

PUNISHMENT

One writer expresses a remarkable theory of the dragon's posthumous state. He says that when they die dragons turn into crabs.

Dragons are punished for minor offenses, according to the will of heaven, by having their ears cut off; for greater offenses, by being sent to the earth, where they are exposed to the view of men in a state as if dead.

DRAGON FAVORS

Three things of which dragons are exceedingly fond are bamboo trees, arsenic, and the flesh of swallows.

BAMBOO

The graceful branches of the bamboo are very pleasing to the eye of the dragon who, when there is no human being in sight, delights to lie under their shade and hear the wind rustling in the leaves above.

ARSENIC

Arsenic, which is to mortal man a deadly poison, is food to the dragon. In fact, it is a favorite article of diet, and dragons grow fat upon it.

SWALLOW FLESH

The delicacy, however, for which the dragon has the greatest fondness, is swallows' flesh. Woe to the man who ever tries to cross a body of water in a boat after having eaten a dish of roasted swallows, for a peculiar fragrance, which dragons are always able to detect, will cling to his person.

The man in the boat will be pursued by one of these animals, who will cause a storm to rise, the boat will be upset, and the unfortunate person will fall into the water, where he will fall easy prey to the ruler of the sea.

Under ordinary conditions the dragon shows no fondness for human flesh, but with such provocation we are told that he should be considered entirely excusable.

HIBERNATION

At the autumnal equinox, according to one source, the majority of dragons descend into the sea where they hibernate for six months.

In fact, the home of dragons is on the floor of the ocean where they dwell in beautiful palaces. At the vernal (spring) equinox dragons leave the sea and ascend again into the clouds.

Destructive typhoons and hurricanes along the coast, in the spring and autumn, are caused by the disturbance of the waters when the great animals enter or leave their water home.

THE "DRAGON SQUARE"

This insignia of rank was worn on a gown by the great statesman Li Hongzhang (formerly romanized as Li Hung Chang). All Manchu officials carried, upon the front and the back of their robes of state, richly embroidered squares like this. The gowns of civil officers bore pictures of birds, while those of military officials had animals. Each of the nine ranks in both series employed its own distinguishing emblem. The dragon was worn by the prime minister, by princes, and the emperor. Li Hongzhang was prime minister of China for twenty years. The threads are of gold and silver and the background is black satin.

DEITIES RIDING DRAGONS ACROSS THE CLOUDS

(Image from *Researches into Chinese Superstitions* by Henry Dore, S.J., 1938)

CHAPTER EIGHT:
HOW DRAGONS CONTROL THE FORTUNES OF MEN

DRAGON PATHS

The surface of the earth is believed to be covered with a network of invisible paths of the dragon known as *Lung Mei*. People who build their houses or find graves for their dead upon one of these courses are extremely fortunate.

The ruling emperors, however, made efforts to prevent their subjects from occupying the positions upon such auspicious sites.

When Emperor Taizu, the founder of the Song[26] dynasty, while still an unknown young man in reduced financial straits, was forced to move his father's bones, he carried them in a reed bag and buried them by accident upon one of these dragon paths. As a result of this fact, we are told, heaven smiled upon him and he himself not long afterward became an emperor.

---

[26] Formerly romanized as the Sung dynasty.

EMPEROR TAIZU

CLOUD FORMATION

When Chinese observe the natural phenomenon, which in the West is commonly described as "the sun drawing up water,"[27] they say that what is seen is the dragon sucking up water to form the clouds.

RAINFALL

When rain falls upon one man's field and not upon his neighbor's, or upon one half of a man's farm and not upon the other, one explanation that is advanced for this fact is that the line which marks the division of dry and wet land is directly beneath the boundary line of the territory governed by two different dragons. One sees fit to order rain when the other does not.

The territories controlled by the different dragons are redistributed once each year, on the seventeenth of the third month, which is known as *Li Hsia*, "The Festival of the Beginning of Summer."

OTHER STORIES

A few amusing illustrations of the way in which dragon superstitions have been allowed to play a leading part in Chinese life have come to the writer's attention.

OFFICIAL CHANGED INTO A DRAGON

A Tianjin district magistrate, about forty years ago, tried to make an outlet from the Hai River[28] in order to turn off the water at the

---

[27] Crepuscular rays, also known as God Rays, formed by are rays of sunlight that stream through gaps in clouds.
[28] Previously called Bai He in Chinese, meaning "White River", formerly romanized as Pei Ho in English.

time of a flood. After spending too much money in what proved to be an unsuccessful effort, he jumped into the river and was drowned.

The story goes that the flood immediately subsided and the official turned into a dragon. Shortly afterwards he was changed into a snake and was captured. This creature was carried in state into Tianjin City where it was placed in the dragon temple and was worshiped by the viceroy of Zhili province[29], who was none other than Li Hung Chang. This official later became prime minister and held that position for twenty years.

THE DRAGON HILL

In the heart of Wuchang[30] there is a steep hill that cuts the business part of the city into two sections. This hill is so steep that it is practically impossible to carry the traffic over it. Some Chinese claim the hill to be the dwelling place of a tortoise, others of a serpent, and still others of a dragon.

Some years ago, when Chang Chili Tung was living in that city as viceroy of Hunan and Hubei[31] provinces, he caused a tunnel to be cut through the hill so that communication from one business center to the other would be facilitated. Not long after this was completed, the viceroy began to suffer from a carbuncle on his neck.

Chinese and foreign physicians alike failed in their attempts to cure him. At last a geomancer was consulted, who said without hesitation,

> I know the reason for your Excellency's illness. You have caused the dragon's haunt to be penetrated. Block up the tunnel in the hill and you will get well.

---

[29] Zhili, formerly romanized as Chih-li, was a province in northern China until it was dissolved in 1928 during the era of the Republic of China.
[30] One of the three cities that merged into the capital of Hubei province, Wuhan.
[31] Formerly romanized as Hupeh.

The thing was done, the viceroy soon recovered, and faith in the dragon on the part of the people of Wuchang was more firmly established than ever.

HAPPY DRAGON IMPROVES ACADEMIC RESULTS

Many years ago large numbers of the students of Hangzhou[32] City failed to pass the *Chu Jen*, or Master of Arts, Examination. The fact sorely puzzled the city magistrates, who 'lost much face.'

No explanation could be found for this fact until a geomancer explained that a dragon living in the mountain range northwest of the city had no room to wag his head, and that a large section of one end of the range must be dug away before Hangzhou students would be able to succeed.

The geomancer's suggestion was carried out, the dragon was given the chance he desired, and it is needless to say that since that time all has been well.

---

[32] Formerly romanized as Hangchow City.

EMPEROR KANGXI ON THE DRAGON THRONE

Kangxi was the second emperor of the Manchu dynasty. He ascended the throne at the age of eight and ruled China for over sixty years. This portrait was once preserved in the imperial galleries of the Manchu rulers.

A DRAGON LANTERN

The fifteenth day of the first month of the Chinese year is known as the "Feast of Lanterns." For centuries Chinese in many parts of the country have observed the evening of the fifteenth with lantern parades. One of the most spectacular of the lanterns usually exhibited is made in the form of a huge dragon.

Before the Republic was established dragon lanterns were not infrequently seventy-five to one hundred feet in length. These were supported by from twenty-five to thirty men. Occasionally these lanterns were used at other times of the year, more particularly on the fifth of the fifth month of the lunar calendar, a holiday known as the "Dragon Boat Festival."

A DRAGON BOAT RACE IN FUZHOU

This copy of an old engraving depicts a huge "dragon boat" passing gracefully up the Min River at Fuzhou. Approximately forty rowers paddle the long craft, which glides swiftly up the river to the music of drums and gongs.

CHAPTER NINE:
THE HOLD OF THE DRAGON ON CHINA

DRAGON NAMES

The word "dragon" occupies a prominent place in the common phraseology of the country. Some illustrations of this fact are as follows:

> Deaf people are called "lung,"' a character formed by the combination of the dragon and ear characters signifying a person with ears like a dragon (which we are informed is deaf).
>
> The asparagus plant is known as "dragon's beard grass."
>
> The gentian flower is called the "dragon's gall."[33]

---

[33] Gentian is called *lung tan*, or dragon's gall, due to its very bitter taste.

A common variety of pine is known as "dragon's tail pine," from the supposed similarity of its branches to the tail of the dragon.

Amaryllis lilies and also the blossoms of a certain locust tree are called "dragon's claw flowers." This is no doubt on account of the shape of the flower clusters.

Fire engines are called "water dragons."

Locomotives and water faucets are commonly designated as "dragon heads."

The keel of a ship goes by the name of the "dragon bone." Water spouts are known as "Mangling dragons." The name was probably given them by junkmen and fishermen who considered these to be the tails of dragons suspended from the clouds.

Spirited horses are said to have "dragon dispositions."

Betrothal certificates are known as "dragon-phoenix papers."

Wedding cakes are called "dragon-phoenix cakes."

The published list of Master of Arts graduates was known as the "Dragon-Tiger Register."

DRAGON AND PHOENIX MOTIF

GEOGRAPHY

A large number of cities, prefectures, rivers, and mountains have the character "dragon" incorporated into their names. One of the largest rivers of Manchuria[34] and one of its three provinces are named *Hei Lung Kiang* (Black Dragon River)[35], because it is related that a large black dragon once made its appearance in its waters.

One of the most famous mountains of the province of Jiangxi[36] is known as the "Dragon-Tiger Mountain."

DRAGON-TIGER MOUNTAIN, JIANGXI PROVINCE

---

[34] The historical name, Manchuria, now commonly refers to Northeast China.
[35] Now called Heilong Jiang River, it forms the border between Northeastern China and the Russian Far East, where it is called the Amur river.
[36] Formerly romanized as Kiangsi province.

THE GATEWAY TO THE DRAGON WELL

Situated four or five miles west of the city of Hangzhou is the center of the district that gives its name to what is perhaps the most famous tea in China. This is known as "Long Jing." The tea takes its name from a pool of water called "The Dragon Well." The walls of a monastery surround the pool. This photograph shows the entrance to the temple grounds. The two characters over the arch form one of the best-known names in all China.

In the excellent new encyclopedia issued by the Commercial Press at the time of this book's first publication in 1912, there are no less than 257 references to the dragon. Fifty-one of these are the names of cities or villages, twenty-four of mountains and rivers, and fifteen the names of flora of various genera.

DRAGON'S WELL TEA

Perhaps the most popular kind of tea in China is the "Dragon's Well Tea." This received its designation from the fact that its original home was in a valley of *Long Jing*[37], Dragon's Well.

Among the hills on the farther shores of Hangzhou's beautiful West Lake is nestled a monastery, on the estate of which is a pool of crystal-clear water. From the depths of this "well" a dragon was once seen to rise. The "Dragon's Well" is now the name of the monastery and also of the surrounding hills.

Tea of this name, though it may never have grown near Hangzhou, is as highly prized in distant Sichuan[38] and in other distant parts of China as it is in the capital of Zhejiang[39] province.

IMPERIAL USAGE

The emperor's most reverential title was "The True Dragon," and in harmony with that idea the word "dragon" in the adjectival sense was used in names of all that had to do with his life and position.

As an example of this his throne was the "dragon's seat," his hands the "dragon's claws," the pen he used was the "dragon's brush," the imperial robes were called "dragon's garments," and the imperial glance was known as "dragon's eyes."

---

[37] Formerly romanized as Lung Ching.
[38] Formerly romanized as Szechwan province.
[39] Formerly romanized as Chekiang province.

The "Dragon Tablet" was the name given to the imperial tablet, which was worshiped during the Qing dynasty in every large temple and monastery in the land, and even in mosques. The inscription on the tablet read as follows:

> To the reigning Emperor. May he live ten thousand years, ten thousand years, ten thousand times ten thousand years.

The tablet received its name from the fact that it represented the Emperor, "The True Dragon," and because it bore at its top a dragon's head.

OFFICIAL INSIGNIA

One insignia of official rank, before the Revolution, was the picture-square embroidered in gold and silver thread and worn on the front and back of official robes.

The squares worn by civil officers bore the pictures of birds, while those of military officials were decorated with the pictures of animals; each rank and grade having its corresponding variety of bird or beast.

The emperor, the princes, and the prime minister were allowed the special privilege of wearing the dragon on one of these embroidered squares.

THE CHINESE DRAGON FLAG

The round disk on the Chinese Dragon Flag[40], which is often pictured before the mouth of the dragon, is explained by some as a pearl, by others as a huge spider metamorphosed into a ball. We are repeatedly told in fables that dragons have a peculiar fondness

---

[40] The dragon appeared on national flags during the Qing dynasty.

THE DRAGON TABLET

During the Manchu dynasty, practically every Buddhist and Taoist temple of any size had an imperial dragon tablet in a prominent place upon the altar. Usually this stood before the image. The words it bore were these: "To the reigning emperor. May he live ten thousand years, ten thousand years, ten thousand times ten thousand years." In the gilded decoration about the characters three dragons twine themselves. This photograph was taken in Hangzhou in March, 1922. The tablet stands on the altar in the Temple of the Great Buddha, which is situated upon the north edge of the West Lake.

for teasing spiders. A more satisfactory theory, however, is that the disk represents the sun.

According to this explanation, the dragon is not trying to devour that heavenly body, as some would lead us to suppose, but is gazing with a great longing, for it desires to become like the sun in brilliance.

In referring to the Dragon Flag, the fact is worthy of notice that although this design appeared upon Chinese military banners through many centuries, the selection of the dragon emblem as a national insignia was of comparatively recent date. It is probable that the custom of foreign nations of using national emblems had a large part to play with the adoption of a national flag.

THE DRAGON FLAG

There is a feeling among many friends of China, and even among a few Chinese as well, that the effect of the Revolution and the passing of the Dragon Flag will very shortly kill out the dragon idea. This the writer believes is impossible.

CONTINUATION OF THE CHINESE DRAGON

A belief that has gripped the nation for over forty centuries is not to be shaken even by an historic revolution, which, though cataclysmic in itself, yet in relation to the ages which have passed, is little more than a ripple upon the surface of the sea of time.

The dragon is neither a symbol of the Manchu dynasty nor a type of absolute monarchy, and has nothing in common with either. The idea is distinctly a heritage of the Chinese race itself, and as such it will probably live as long as this people.

It will survive at least until a generation after Western science has permeated and dominated every seaside village, every mountain hamlet, and every inland city, to the remotest bounds and limits of this vast Middle Kingdom[41].

---

[41] The Chinese word for China, *Zhongguo*, translates to 'Middle Kingdom'.

Printed in Great Britain
by Amazon